Introduction

The Fleam Dyke and Roman Road W
incorporating two of Cambridgeshire
gently undulating countryside comp
farmland and it skirts a number of a
nature reserve. There are extensive v

Both Fleam Dyke and the Roman Road are archaeological sites of national importance, and large sections of each are scheduled monuments. At approximately 6 km in length and surviving to over 4m above field level and over 8m from ditch to bank in places, Fleam Dyke is the second largest of a series of four banked and ditched linear earthworks that cross Cambridgeshire. From an elevation of 15m above sea level at the fen edge, the dyke rises gradually as it travels southeast, reaching an elevation of 90m above sea level at the Ambush.

The dykes were constructed in the early Anglo-Saxon period (5th - 7th centuries AD) to act as territorial markers and defensive barriers between the kingdoms of East Anglia and Mercia. Modern excavations have revealed that Fleam Dyke underwent at least three phases of construction and repair before finally going out of use during the 7th century AD.

The Roman Road runs from Worts' Causeway past Worsted Lodge Farm towards Horseheath, and represents the longest surviving stretch of Roman Road in Cambridgeshire. The name 'Via Devana' was invented by an eighteenth century historian, who assumed that the road ran between Colchester and Chester, known as Deva in Roman times. In fact, this section of the Roman Road network probably follows the route of a prehistoric trackway that continued in use into the Roman period, linking the small town at Cambridge with the Icknield Way and beyond. After the end of the Roman Empire in the 5th century, the route continued in use by travellers and in particular the wool merchants of Suffolk, giving rise to its old name of 'Worsted Street' or 'Wool Street'.

Flowers on Fleam Dyke.

Fleam Dyke near the A11, looking Southeast.

Excavations in the 1990s demonstrated that the road was flanked by ditches on either side, and that the gravel road surface was raised on a foundation of compacted chalk, known as the *agger*. The raised *agger* can still be seen along some sections of the Roman Road, particularly the stretch from Wandlebury to Worsted Lodge.

Parts of both Fleam Dyke and the Roman Road are Sites of Special Scientific Interest (SSSI), well known for their chalk grassland flora and fauna. Once, much of Cambridgeshire between the fens and the clay-capped ground to the southeast was covered with chalk grassland grazed by sheep. Over the last 200 years, most of this area was ploughed to grow arable crops and relatively little survives, the only remnants being areas that were impractical to farm such as parts of the Roman Road, the Devil's Dyke and Fleam Dyke.

Grazing by sheep and subsequently by a high population of rabbits maintained the chalk grassland flowers, but following the spread of myxomatosis in the 1950s, both sites became increasingly covered in scrub. In recent years, however, large areas have been cleared and the situation is gradually

Greater Knapweed (left), Marjoram (centre) and Kidney Vetch (right).

The Roman Road near Copley Hill.

improving. In selected parts, the grassland is now mown regularly and the grass cuttings are removed to reduce nutrient levels and encourage wild flowers.

In spring, some of the first flowers to be seen are violets and cowslips. From May onwards, there is a succession of low growing plants typical of chalk grassland including the common rock rose, horseshoe vetch, wild thyme, milkwort and eyebright. As the summer progresses, lady's bedstraw forms a background to the mauve, purple and blue of knapweeds, small scabious, field scabious, clustered bellflowers and harebells together with salad burnet, dropwort, restharrow, ploughman's-spikenard and cat-mint. Greater knapweed may be accompanied by its parasite, knapweed broomrape and the semi-parasitic yellow rattle is common. Large patches of starry white squinancywort can also be seen. Here and there you will find bright pink sainfoin and an occasional pyramidal orchid.

Also on Fleam Dyke, between the A11 and Bedford Gap are nine juniper bushes, the only examples of our native juniper, *Juniperus communis*, which remain in East Anglia. Some small seedlings, the first for many years, are in protective guards and two plantations of cuttings near the A11 are well established.

Rock Rose (left), Dropwort (centre) and Clustered Bellflower (right).

Horseshoe Vetch (left); Horseshoe Vetch and Milkwort (right).

The variety of flowers brings a profusion of insects. Butterflies are one of the main attractions and more than 20 species have been recorded on both sites. The majority are fairly common, widespread species but some of these such as the meadow brown, gatekeeper and brimstone can often be seen in large numbers. Unfortunately, many species associated more specifically with chalk grassland such as the grizzled skipper, marbled white, grayling, small blue and chalkhill blue disappeared when the dyke became covered with scrub. However, on Fleam Dyke, chalkhill blues have recently been recorded and it is hoped that a colony will become re-established. Similarly, on the Roman Road, marbled whites were recorded in 2007 for the first time in many years. In May, another less common species, the green hairstreak can be seen on Fleam Dyke between Fulbourn and Mutlow Hill, often basking in the sunshine in the remaining areas of scrub. Colourful day-flying moths such as the five-spot burnet and cinnabar are sometimes seen during the summer months.

Other insects include bumblebees, a range of solitary bees and wasps, hoverflies, beetles, crickets and grasshoppers. The numerous anthills, particularly on Fleam Dyke, are evidence of large numbers of meadow ants, which are only found in areas of old and undisturbed grassland.

Among the mammals, rabbits are common and hares can often be seen. Foxes, badgers, muntjac and fallow deer, weasels, stoats and numerous small mammals are also present. Common lizards can sometimes be seen basking in the sun and occasionally there have been sightings of grass snakes.

A wide range of bird species can be seen and heard on the walk including whitethroat, yellowhammer, corn bunting, skylark, meadow pipit, long-tailed tit, linnet, fieldfare and many more. Perhaps the most spectacular are the buzzard and red kite which have both recently returned to the area and can sometimes be seen flying overhead.

Male Chalkhill Blue (left), and male Brimstone (right).

Walk information

Distance
40km (25 miles). See below for shorter walk options.

Terrain
Generally well-maintained footpaths, bridleways and byways through gently undulating countryside. There are three cross-field paths at the southeast end of the route which may be muddy after rain but can be avoided by taking a short-cut along the eastern edge of Hare Wood.

Accessibility
The Roman Road from Worts' Causeway to Horseheath is generally accessible to wheelchairs and mobility scooters but some parts may be muddy in winter or wet weather. Other parts of the route are not readily accessible.

Maps
Ordnance Survey Explorer Maps 209 and 210; Landranger Map 154.

The route uses public rights of way shown on the above maps, which are updated on a regular basis. Paths are very occasionally diverted, and while diversions are generally signed on the ground, more recent changes and any temporary path closures can be checked on the Cambridgeshire County Council website at www.cambridgeshire.gov.uk/countryside.

Route updates may also be published on the Friends of the Roman Road and Fleam Dyke website: www.frrfd.org.uk

Start / finish point
Start of Roman Road on Worts' Causeway at OS Grid Reference TL 493547.

Car Parking
There is a small parking area at the start of the walk **(A)** but preferred alternatives are as follows.

Babraham Road 'Park and Ride' (B) (Entrance at TL 480545), approximately 1.5km from the starting point.

At the time of writing the 'Park and Ride' is open from 7am to 8pm Monday to Friday, 8am to 8pm on Saturdays and approximately 9am to 7pm on Sundays and Bank Holidays. Cycle racks are provided. For up to date information check on the website: www.cambridgeshire.gov.uk/transport/around/parkandride

Take the permissive path from the rear of the parking area to the crossroads of Worts' Causeway and Limekiln Road. Follow the permissive route inside the roadside hedge to the Beechwoods Nature Reserve and then continue along the road to the start of the walk.

Green Hairstreak (left), and male Gatekeeper (right).

Magog Down car park (C) (TL 486532) (free at the time of writing) and **Wandlebury car park (D)** (TL 492532) (charge), both approximately 3km from the start.

From these car parks it is possible to walk through Wandlebury Country Park and join the Roman Road at TL 505536.

Car parking is also available in a number of villages on or near the route, including Fulbourn and Balsham.

Public Transport

There are frequent bus services from Cambridge City centre to the Babraham Road Park and Ride. Buses run every 10 to 15 minutes and the approximate journey time is 18 minutes. For further information consult: www.cambridgeshire.gov.uk/transport/around/parkandride/

Citi1, 2 and 7 buses serve Addenbrooke's Hospital, from which it is possible to walk along Wort's Causeway to the start of the walk (approximately 2.5km).

Stagecoach Bus Service 13 from Cambridge to Haverhill stops at Wandlebury. Bus Services 16 and 17 serve Fulbourn and Service 16 continues to Haverhill via Balsham, West Wratting, West Wickham and Withersfield.

Call 01223 717740 for details of bus services or consult the following website for further information and timetables: www.cambridgeshire.gov.uk/transport/around/buses/

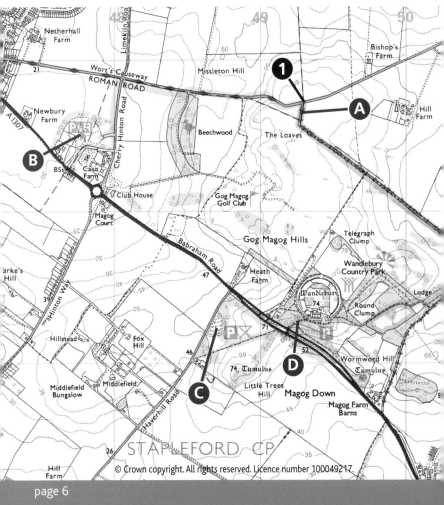

Route directions

The route can be walked in either a clockwise or an anticlockwise direction. The following description follows the route in a clockwise direction. The paths along both the Roman Road and Fleam Dyke are very easy to follow and require few directions. Routes linking the two linear sites, particularly in the southeast, are given in more detail. Places of interest along the route, which are described in a separate section of this booklet, are marked in bold lettering.

From the starting point **(1)** proceed SE along the Roman Road for approximately 3km passing on your right a golf course, **Wandlebury Country Park** and Copley Hill, a tree-covered natural chalk knoll on private land, on which is a Bronze Age burial mound, one of several examples on the South Cambridgeshire chalklands.

About 600m after passing the top of Copley Hill, at the end of a row of beech trees on the left and approximately 20m before a similar row on the right at TL 517528, turn left (N) onto a footpath **(2)**. This path follows a field edge and leads through an attractive strip of woodland. After emerging from the trees, continue on the field-edge path for about 600m to a short cross-field section, after which the path runs to the left of a hedge and a deep ditch before reaching a busy road at TL 525552 **(3)**, about 2.5km from where

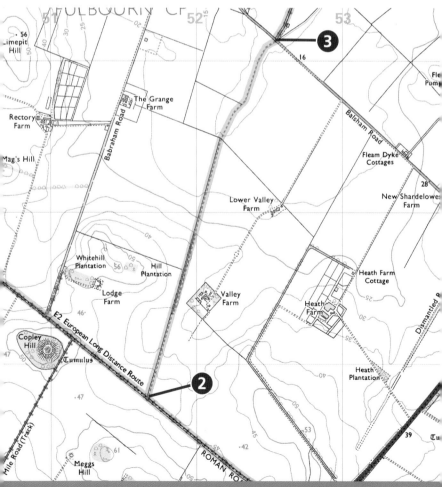

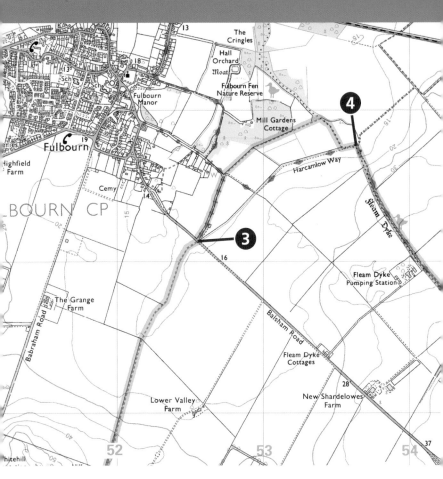

it left the Roman Road. From here, the village of **Fulbourn** can be reached quite easily and it is only a short distance to the White Hart pub.

Cross the road and continue N on a public byway. After 500m, cross another track (Stonebridge Lane) and pass through some bollards, onto a footpath. This path crosses two footbridges and then runs NE along the side of **Fulbourn Fen Nature Reserve**, which can be accessed by turning left over a footbridge at TL 532559. About 200m beyond this point the path bears right (SE) and follows a stream for 250m, before crossing another bridge to a track. Turn left on the track and then right, following the sign to Fleam Dyke **(4)**, and continue in a SE direction.

Ascend the steps onto the bank of Fleam Dyke and proceed along the top of the bank passing the **Fleam Dyke Pumping Station** on the right after 900m and then crossing the route of the disused **Chesterford to Newmarket Railway** after another 500m. The path then passes **Mutlow Hill,** another Bronze Age burial mound, and shortly afterwards reaches a concrete farm road, beyond which is a footbridge over the A11, about 50m to the right. Over the bridge, a tarmac path beside the main road leads back to the line of the dyke. The footpath then follows a very open stretch of the dyke for 800m, with areas of typical chalk grassland flora, to a gap in the dyke known as Bedford Gap, which was cut in 1763. The route then becomes thickly wooded. Pass through Dungate Farm and where the path forks at the Ambush, one of the highest points on the dyke, bear left and follow the residual line of the Dyke.

Fleam Dyke between the A11 and Bedford Gap, looking Southeast.

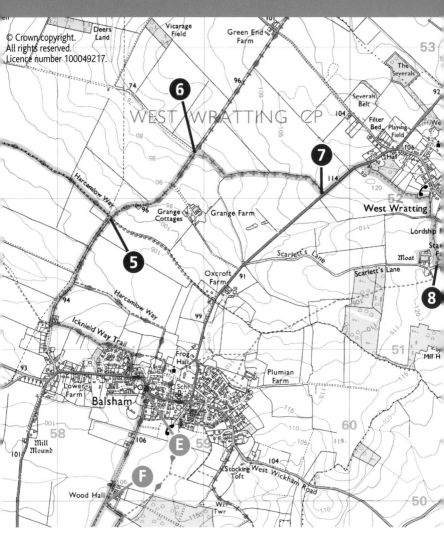

After a further 1.5km, reach a byway at TL 583519, which forms part of the **Icknield Way Path (5)**. A right turn (S) at this point will lead to the village of **Balsham** with its two pubs (for directions see 'Options for shorter walks'). To continue the main route, turn left in a NE direction, and after walking 700m, turn right by a clump of trees **(6)**. Follow this byway E for about 1km to the road **(7)**. Turn left (NE) along the road towards **West Wratting**. After 300m, turn right (S) onto a track for 50m, then left to a footpath, which skirts the edge of the village on your left. At a T-junction in front of a fence, by turning left, a short diversion can be made into the village and the Chestnut Tree public house. Otherwise turn right towards the S following the fence and then a ditch on your left until you come to a bridge over the ditch after 400m. Continue to the road from Scarlett's Farm and turn left **(8)**.

At the E end of this road turn right into Mill Road. After 200m, take the signed footpath to the left (SE) past the grain store. 150m beyond the grain store this footpath joins a metalled farm road on the edge of West Wratting Park. The road goes through a small wood and then heads SE beside a tall hedge on the left for 250m. The concrete and the hedge then end but a track continues E for another 250m to a corner, where it turns N beside another hedge on the left for 100m to a junction at TL 616512 **(9)**.

Turn right (E) at this junction and follow the path along field-edges, going E to the first field corner, then S. At the next corner go through a gap in the thick hedge and continue ahead, passing Rand's Wood on your left. The path then turns right along the field edge for 200m to a junction. Do not cross the footbridge but bear left along a short, grassy lane between hedges. The path then skirts round to the right of a garden to reach the road at Burton End, **West Wickham (10)**, a distance of about 2km from Mill Road.

Turn left (E) and after about 50m, turn right onto a short cross-field path, then left (E) along another cross-field path which leads to a well defined footpath with high hedges leading to Leys Wood. Alternatively, to avoid the cross-field paths, continue along the road for a further 300m and then right onto the path leading S to Leys Wood.

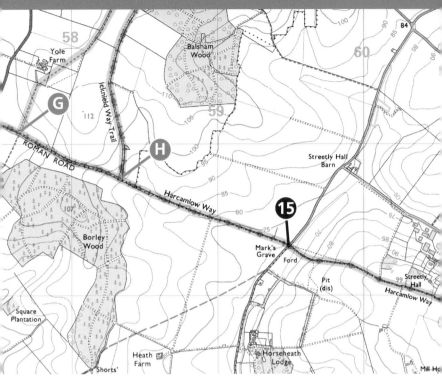

Bear right (W) around the edge of Leys Wood to Hill Farm **(11)**. Turn left past the farm buildings and after a short path (S) across the corner of an arable field, join a wide grassy path leading SE beside a hedge on your right to the edge of Ash Plantation. Continue S along a short cross-field path to the corner of Hare Wood **(12)**. The directions from Hill Farm to Hare Wood describe paths as generally walked in this area at the time of writing, some of which do not fully correspond to the line on the Definitive Map and hence to the line on the OS map. The Definitive line may be more available when you come to walk this section.

As a short cut and to avoid further cross-field paths continue straight on along the side of Hare Wood to rejoin the walk at TL 624476 **(14)**. This shortens the walk by about 3km.

To do the complete walk, turn left (E) at the corner of Hare Wood along the field edge for 300m and then bear slightly left on a cross-field path to Over Wood. Cross a footbridge, walk through a corner of the wood and follow the footpath right (SW) for 150m and then left (SE) where, after 200m, it crosses the Suffolk boundary and continues over a footbridge and around field edges on your right to the **Withersfield** road **(13)**. The town of Haverhill can be seen less than 2km away.

Turn right and walk S along the road for about 250m to where it starts to bend right and descend more steeply. Turn right again through trees and onto a cross-field path which is the start of the route heading W along the Roman Road. Behind you there are more obvious signs of the Roman Road towards Haverhill but this is not a public right of way.

450m from the road, go over a bridge and cross a track into a small wooded area. Head W across another arable field and bear right along a track which follows the edge of a field for 600m to the SE corner of Hare Wood **(14)**. The

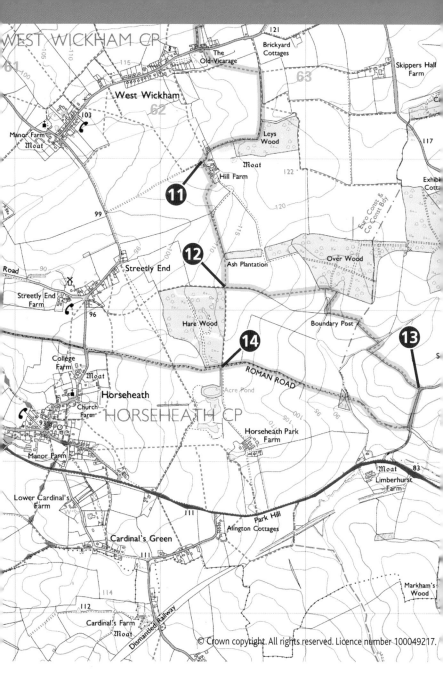

track appears to be the route generally walked at the time of writing but does not correspond to the line on the Definitive Map and hence to the line on the OS map, which goes to the left of the hedge on the opposite side from the track. The Definitive path may be more available when you come to walk this section. From the corner of Hare Wood the Roman Road runs through the former **Horseheath Park**.

It is now a wide track which skirts N of the village of **Horseheath** and crosses the Horseheath to West Wickham road. A path to the left before this road leads into the village with its pub, the Red Lion. Continue along the Roman Road and cross the Bartlow to West Wratting road 2km W of Horseheath at Mark's Grave **(15)**. The origin of this name is unknown.

After another 2km, the Roman Road crosses the Linton to Balsham road **(16)**, where **Chilford Hall** vineyard lies a short distance to the S. 1.5km further on, it crosses the Hildersham to Balsham road **(17)**, and reaches the bridge over the A11 at Worsted Lodge **(18)** after another 4km. Diversions into the villages of **Linton** and **Hildersham** are possible.

About 1.4km after Worsted Lodge, the Roman Road rejoins the outward route **(2)** at the beech trees that mark the turnoff towards Fulbourn and returns to the start (see pages 6-7).

The Roman Road near Hildersham, looking Northwest.

Options for shorter walks

Paths linking Fleam Dyke and the Roman Road through the village of Balsham can be used to divide the walk into two approximately equal parts.

To do the northwestern part from Wort's Causeway, a total of 28km (17 miles), follow the above directions to the byway at TL 583519 (point **5** on the combined route). Turn right to the village, which can be reached by continuing along Fox Road or by turning left on either of two footpaths leading to the recreation ground and church. Cross the High Street at the village green, close to the Black Bull pub and enter Woodhall Lane **(E)**. After 750m leave the byway, which turns to the left, and go straight ahead onto a footpath, passing Yole Farm **(F)**. Continue S across fields towards Rivey Hill water tower to join the Roman Road at TL 577491 **(G)**. Turn right and follow the Roman Road back to the start of the walk.

A shorter version of the northwestern part of the walk with a distance of 22km (14 miles) can be done from Balsham, omitting the 3km of the Roman Road from Wort's Causeway to the junction with the footpath to Fulbourn at TL 517528 (combined route, point **2**), 1.4km from Worsted Lodge and immediately before a row of beech trees on the right. There is parking in Balsham near the church. This part of the walk could also be done from Fulbourn, where there is limited parking at the end of Stonebridge Lane near the main entrance to the Nature Reserve.

The village of Balsham can also be used as a starting point for the southeastern part of the walk, a distance of 20km (12.5 miles). From the village, take Fox Road and continue past the footpath from Fleam Dyke to follow directions given for the complete walk. Returning along the Roman Road and after entering a wooded area, turn right at TL 584488 **(H)** by the last power pole on your right onto a byway to Balsham.

Links with other long-distance walks

Icknield Way Path

The Icknield Way, claimed to be the oldest road in Britain, comprised a series of prehistoric tracks running along the chalk 'spine' of England. The current waymarked long-distance path extends 206km (128 miles) from Knettishall Heath in Suffolk to Ivinghoe Beacon in Buckinghamshire, linking Peddars Way with the Ridgeway.

It crosses the southeastern end of Fleam Dyke near Balsham and, at its central point, passes through the village and links with the Roman Road near Borley Wood. After following the Roman Road for a short distance, it turns south into the village of Linton. The Icknield Way between Fleam Dyke and the Roman Road is one of the routes recommended in the section on 'Options for shorter walks'.

Harcamlow Way

The Harcamlow Way (identified on some OS maps but not waymarked) is a 227km (141 mile) route, devised in the 1970s by members of the Essex Ramblers' Association, which starts and finishes in Harlow, Essex and follows a figure of eight with a northernmost point in Cambridge. It incorporates the whole length of Fleam Dyke, links with the Roman Road through Balsham and passes through the village of Horseheath.

Places of interest on or close to the walk

Wandlebury Country Park

Wandlebury Country Park was established by the Cambridge Preservation Society following the purchase of the Wandlebury Estate in 1954. The park includes areas of chalk grassland and beech woodland, and is open daily for recreation and public enjoyment. Within the park, and occupying the crest of the Gog Magog hills, is Wandlebury Camp, a circular hill fort dating to the Mid-Late Iron Age (c. 400 BC - AD 42). Hill forts are enclosed settlements, which are surrounded by single or multiple banks and ditches, and traditionally thought to have had a defensive function. Several skeletons have been found at Wandlebury, some showing signs of injury.

Excavations in 1955-6 showed that Wandlebury Camp was first constructed in the 4th century BC, after which time it fell out of use, before being refortified with a double bank and ditch in the1st century BC. Postholes and storage pits found within the ramparts also provided evidence of occupation within the hill fort. More recently, excavations by the University of Cambridge in the 1990s have shown that the hill fort was preceded by a large open settlement, and worked flints recovered in the vicinity indicate a human presence at Wandlebury since the 3rd millennium BC.

During the 18th century the interior was converted into a racing lodge by the Earl of Godolphin, and an extensive stable block, clock tower and mansion were constructed within the earthwork defences. The inner rampart and ditch were later levelled to make way for gardens during the 19th century. Gogmagog House was demolished in the 1950s, but the grade II listed stable block and clock tower survive to this day.

Also located within the hill fort is a timber-framed granary, dating to the early 15th century. The granary was dismantled from its original location in Tadlow, in southwest Cambridgeshire, and erected at its current location by the Cambridge Preservation Society in 1981.

Fulbourn

Fulbourn, with its three pubs and small shopping centre, is a large village with a population of around 5000. It lies just to the east of the walk and has a number of attractive thatched houses and a restored smock windmill originally built in 1808.

Wandlebury: the ditch (left), and stable clock (right).

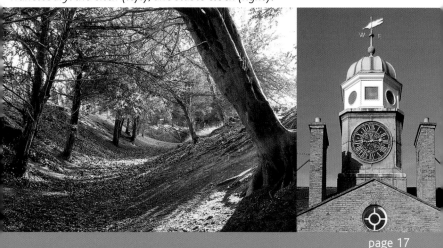

Fulbourn village centre (left), and Church of St Vigor (right).

The church of St Vigor, around which an early settlement was built, lies on a direct route from the Roman Road to the fens. Fulbourn Manor, which is close to the church was first built in the 17th century and was surrounded by a small park. The house and park were both greatly enlarged in the early 19th century and a new front was added in the early 20th century.

More recent development of the village has taken place mainly to the west of the village centre towards Cambridge. The Roman Road and Fleam Dyke form parts of the parish boundary.

Fulbourn Fen Nature Reserve

Fulbourn Fen Nature Reserve, located on the eastern side of the village, covers approximately 70 acres, the majority of which is an SSSI. The Reserve area is divided approximately equally between woodland and meadowland. The Reserve can be entered from its eastern side directly from the Fleam Dyke and Roman Road Walk or, alternatively, from the village at the car parking area near the end of Stonebridge Lane.

The Reserve land is part of the Fulbourn Manor Estate and is managed by the Wildlife Trust on a long-term contract. Originally fen, the site has been drained and has a much lower water table than in the past. There are still remnants of alder woodland (which is being enhanced by judicious management) and of secondary woodland that has developed as the wetland has dried out. Non-native trees have been planted in the southern block of woodland, but there are still primrose, wood avens, bugle, stinking hellebore and wood violet in the ground flora.

Four ancient meadows grow on the chalky loam and peat. One, Moat Meadow, was named for the remains of Dunmows Manor, a moated medieval manor house. Recent excavations of the interior have revealed traces of timber and stone buildings dating to the 13th to 17th centuries AD. The meadows, including Ox Meadow and Long Fen, are grazed by cattle as an important part of the management practice and are very rich in flowering plants. Of

Fulbourn Fen Nature Reserve.

special note are the orchids, namely pyramidal, bee, common spotted, common twayblade and southern marsh orchids, but an abundance of cowslips, bird's-foot trefoil, yarrow, salad burnet, adder's tongue, harebell, common gromwell and stinking iris are also to be found. East Fen Pasture, also grazed in summer, is normally partially flooded in winter by raising a sluice and is therefore very wet but there is a boardwalk across the wettest areas. Stoat, weasel and muntjac deer are to be seen as well as kestrel, sparrow hawk and the occasional snipe or mallard during winter.

Fleam Dyke Pumping Station

Fleam Dyke Pumping Station was built between 1912 and 1921 to meet the growing demands for piped water. By 1954 it supplied two thirds of the old county of Cambridgeshire's water. Parts of the original steam machinery were preserved when the pumping station was electrified in 1976. These items, including a sight gauge, are held at the Cambridge Museum of Technology, 01233 368650, info@museumoftechnology.com.

Great Chesterford to Newmarket Railway

About 500m south east of Fleam Dyke pumping station, the dyke is cut by the line of the former Great Chesterford to Newmarket railway, which opened in 1848 as part of a direct route from London to Newmarket. However, the stretch between Chesterford and Six Mile Bottom was very short lived, and was dismantled only three years later when the line from Six Mile Bottom to Cambridge was opened, making this one of the earliest closures in British railway history. The footpath crosses the cutting on an embankment, constructed in the late 1930s in order to provide shooting butts for rifle practice in preparation for the coming war.

Mutlow Hill

This is an example of an Early Bronze Age (c. 2500 - 1500 BC) round barrow, a type of funerary monument made up of a conical mound, often surrounded by a circular ditch and covering one or more burials. Barrows often occur together in larger cemeteries, and were frequently sited in prominent positions in the landscape. Aerial photographs indicate the presence of at least three ring ditches in the area surrounding Mutlow Hill, probably the remains of further barrows.

Mutlow Hill.

Balsham village sign.

Excavations were undertaken at Mutlow Hill in 1852 by the famous antiquarian R.C. Neville. The mound was found to contain at least 8 Bronze Age cremations, all contained in pottery vessels. Some of the cremations contained other grave goods, including a bronze pin, faience beads and a bone pin, and cremated plant remains. Neville also found a circular structure of chalk blocks, which he interpreted as the remains of a Roman temple or shrine. A number of Roman coins, brooches and bracelets were discovered around the structure, possibly left as votive offerings to the deities. Like many other barrows, the site was reused again in Saxon and Medieval times as a meeting place, giving rise to its name.

Visible today is the earthwork mound, some 28m across and 3m in height. The mound has an uneven profile, and has been disturbed by excavation and animal activity.

Balsham

Balsham is one of southeast Cambridgeshire's largest parishes with a population in 2001 of 1641. The village is situated on an east-west plateau. The northern boundary of the parish is formed by Fleam Dyke, while the western and southern boundaries follow the line of Roman Roads.

The earliest settlement at Balsham dates to the end of the 10th century. The Anglo-Saxon Chronicle records that in 1010 Balsham was attacked by Danish raiders, massacring the inhabitants of the village. A sign on the village green commemorates the sole survivor of the attack, a man who successfully defended himself in the church tower. During the 13th century the village was granted a weekly market and annual fair, which took place on the High Street. The old school occupies the site of Balsham Hall, a medieval manor house that was built by the Bishop of Ely in the 13th century. The stone coffins of medieval priests can be seen in the churchyard of the Holy Trinity Church.

The Black Bull public house is actually a 17th century coaching inn, which would have provided a stopover point for travellers on the Newmarket to Linton road. The open fields surrounding the parish were enclosed in 1806, giving rise to the agricultural landscape visible today.

West Wratting

West Wratting is a large parish lying to the northeast of Balsham, with a population of 436 recorded in the 2001 census. The southern extent of the parish follows Fleam Dyke.

The early settlement history in West Wratting is poorly understood, though recent finds are gradually filling in some of the gaps. The earliest documentary

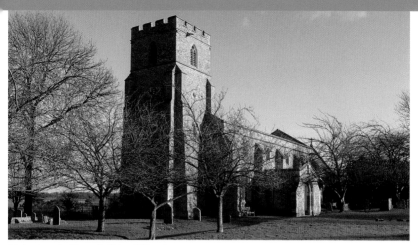

St Andrew's Church, West Wratting.

reference to West Wratting dates from the 10th century, and in 1086 Wratting was recorded as Waratinge, the 'place where cross-wort grows'.

The main manor in the village is West Wratting Hall, situated to the north of St Andrew's Church. The hall is surrounded by parkland (in private ownership), which contains the earthwork remains of a former medieval settlement. A number of other medieval manor houses were scattered around the parish. The walk goes around the perimeter of West Wratting Park with good views of its fine 18th century house.

The open fields around the village were enclosed in 1813, while the large areas of common land at the east end of the parish were used as an airfield during World War II, and are now known as Wratting Common.

West Wickham

The parish of West Wickham is moderately large, with some 423 inhabitants recorded in 2001. The parish is bounded by Worsted Street on the south side.

Archaeological discoveries have shown that the parish was extensively occupied during the Roman period. A villa or tiled building has been identified at Yen Hall, dating from the 2nd to 4th centuries AD. Roman artifacts have also been discovered at Streetly End, suggesting an area of

The Church of St Mary, West Wickham.

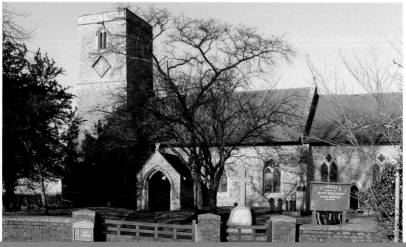

Withersfield Church, door handle.

settlement close to Worsted Street. In 1086 Streetly End was documented as *Stretlaie*, meaning 'wood or clearing by the Roman road'.

Yen Hall was a manorial site and settlement from the 10th century, one of three moated manors in the parish during the medieval period. The church of St Mary dates from the 13th and 14th centuries, from which date it became the main focus of settlement in the village. The open fields surrounding the village were enclosed in 1822.

Withersfield

Withersfield, a pretty Suffolk village close to the southeastern point of the walk is reached by turning left along the road from TL 638475. The White Horse Inn, which is reached before the village itself serves food and has accommodation. The name of the village comes from the ancient practice of enclosing a large area for wether sheep (castrated males kept for their wool).

St Mary's Church, on an ancient crossroads in the centre of the village, is said to be one of the most interesting churches in the area. From the south side it can be seen that the stair turret rises above the battlements of the 15th century tower. Although the design appears to be typical Suffolk perpendicular, in fact almost all of it was built in Victorian times, only the clerestory being medieval. The door handle, with its two dragons, is the oldest survival in the whole building, dating from the 13th century. St Mary's

Horseheath: All Saints Church (left), and village sign (right).

is most famous for its bench ends which line the north ends of the south nave benches. The most easterly is the image of St George defeating the dragon, which writhes in agony beneath the knight's horse's hooves.

Horseheath

Horseheath is a small village with a population of about 450. The Roman Road forms the northern boundary of the parish. The village can be reached from the Roman Road along the metalled road which connects it with West Wickham or there are footpath links both east and west of the village. There are a number of attractive houses around the village centre and the Red Lion pub can be found on the Linton Road to its west. All Saints Church stands on a rise to the north of the village.

East of the village, the Roman Road runs through the former Horseheath Park, the site of Horseheath Hall, an important red-brick country mansion designed by the architect Sir Roger Pratt. The house was surrounded by formal gardens, but was pulled down by the end of the 18th century, when the owners fell into financial difficulty. The wrought iron gates, dating to 1665 and created by one of Wren's foremost sculptors are now at Trinity and St John's Colleges in Cambridge and at Cheveley Rectory, now known as Glebe House. Ponds and earthworks associated with the former landscape park can still be seen from the footpath that passes alongside the site.

Linton

When walking the route in a clockwise direction, the village of Linton can be reached from the Roman Road by turning left onto a waymarked cross-field path just past Borley Wood (TL 576491). Go straight across the first field and diagonally right across the next. At the road, turn left and after 200m, where the road makes a left turn, follow a track which goes straight ahead to the water tower. The path continues down Rivey Hill, with Rivey Wood on the right, into the village.

Set in the Granta valley between rolling hills, Linton has a long history stretching back some 5000 years to Neolithic times. The Romans and the Saxons also had substantial settlements here. The centre, about a half mile square, has been a conservation area for many years with a wealth of 14th – 15th century buildings. The attractive 16th century guildhall, on the banks of the Granta, is close to the parish church.

Linton High Street.

Linton Church (left) and Guildhall from the churchyard (right).

Linton has expanded in recent years and is now a large village with a population of more than 4000. It has three pubs, two of which, the Crown and the Dog and Duck, offer food. There is also an Indian Restaurant and a Chinese take-away.

Chilford Hall

Chilford Hall is home to one of the largest vineyards in East Anglia and is a highly respected wine producer, having earned numerous awards. The vineyard comprises 18 acres of land on a southwest facing slope which lies to the south of the Roman Road. There is a conference centre and a shop and café, which has limited opening hours (see Places to eat and drink). Winery tours are available. The entrance to Chilford Hall is on the route recommended from the Roman Road to the village of Linton just before the track to the water tower.

Hildersham

Another village lying in the Granta valley, Hildersham is a small community of approximately 200 people, centred on the 12th century church and the village pub, The Pear Tree. It is famous for its display of daffodils in the spring. It lies southwest of the Roman Road and can be reached along the minor Hildersham to Balsham road where it crosses the linear site at TL 561498. Alternatively the bridleway, which leaves the Roman Road to the south opposite the track leading to the disused farm buildings called Gunner's Hall at TL 548505, can be used to join the minor road just north of the village.

Further reading

Taylor, Alison (1998). *Archaeology of Cambridgeshire*, Vol. 2: South East Cambridgeshire and the Fen Edge. Cambridgeshire County Council. ISBN 0-902436-50-3.

Chilford Hall: entrance (left) and relief sculpture (right).